Hush Little Baby

A Christmas Song

DON'T WAIT TIL XMAS

Adapted ... be ... man

For
Juliet Eve,

The Sweetest
little child
I know!

ISBN 0-590-45247-9

12 11 10 9 8 7 6 5 4 3 2 1   2 3 4 5 6 7/9

Printed in Singapore.
First Scholastic printing, October 1992.

Hush little darling, don't carry on,
Mama's gonna sing you a Christmas song.

If that Christmas song goes flat,

Mama's gonna get you a pussy cat.

If that pussy cat won't purr,

Papa's gonna get you a Douglas fir.

If that Douglas fir falls down,

Mama's gonna make you a cap and gown.

If that cap and gown don't fit,

Papa's gonna give you a ball and mitt.

If that ball and mitt go astray,

Mama's gonna give you a wind-up sleigh.

If that wind-up sleigh should flip,

Papa's gonna give you a sailing ship.

If that sailing ship won't float,

Mama's gonna give you a downy coat.

If that downy coat gets torn,

Papa's gonna give you a golden horn.

If that golden horn won't blow,

You'll still be the sweetest little child I know.

Hush Little Darling

1. Hush lit-tle dar-ling, don't car-ry on,
2. If that Christ-mas song goes flat,

Ma-ma's gon-na sing you a Christ-mas song.
Ma-ma's gon-na get you a puss-sy cat.

If that pussy cat won't purr,
Papa's gonna get you a Douglas fir.

If that Douglas fir falls down,
Mama's gonna make you a cap and gown.

If that cap and gown don't fit,
Papa's gonna give you a ball and mitt.

If that ball and mitt go a stray,
Mama's gonna give you a wind-up sleigh.

If that wind-up sleigh should flip,
Papa's gonna give you a sailing ship.

If that sailing ship won't float,
Mama's gonna give you a downy coat.

If that downy coat gets torn,
Papa's gonna give you a golden horn.

If that golden horn won't blow,
You'll still be the sweetest little child I know.